Fire Fire!!

Coloured Version

CAROL SUTTERS

AuthorHouse™ UK
1663 Liberty Drive
Bloomington, IN 47403 USA
www.authorhouse.co.uk
UK TFN: 0800 0148641 (Toll Free inside the UK)
UK Local: 02036 956322 (+44 20 3695 6322 from outside the UK)

Because of the dynamic nature of the Internet, any web addresses or links contained in this book may have changed since publication and may no longer be valid. The views expressed in this work are solely those of the author and do not necessarily reflect the views of the publisher, and the publisher hereby disclaims any responsibility for them.

Any people depicted in stock imagery provided by Getty Images are models, and such images are being used for illustrative purposes only.
Certain stock imagery © Getty Images.

This book is printed on acid-free paper.

ISBN: 978-1-6655-8659-7 (sc)
ISBN: 978-1-6655-8658-0 (e)

Library of Congress Control Number: 2021908150

Print information available on the last page.

Published by AuthorHouse 04/23/2021

authorHOUSE®

Today, Tom and Kate have their school friend Hatus come to play with them in their garden. Hatus is from Brazil.

He says to Kate, *"My mum has been really worried about the fires back home where my grandparents live in Brazil. She only just found out yesterday that they are safe. We have been very worried."* Kate replies, *"Fires? I will ask my mum about this."*

Mum sighs, *"Yes, it is terrible that there are wild fires raging in the Amazon rainforest. It is on television."* Just then a special news bulletin on the television showed millions of trees burning in a country called Brazil.

Mum continues, "*Brazil has a famous huge Amazon tropical rain forest which has thousands of trees and these, you will remember from the carbon cycle, are important for producing oxygen.*

This autumn in 2019 over 9500 wildfires are burning across the vast rainforests of Brazil. The fires are out of control and spreading into nearby countries. Some fires are started by humans to clear land for farming and for logs. But the very dry conditions made the fires much worse and unstoppable. This has destroyed large parts of the Amazon forest and damaged the ecosystem. We believe the extreme dry conditions were created due to climate change in the region making the weather more extreme, hotter and drier."

She continues, "*The Amazon rain forest is very important because these trees suck up much carbon dioxide from the air during photosynthesis. This produces about 20% of the world's oxygen. Oxygen is needed for humans and animals to breathe and live. It is really important to preserve the Amazon rainforest. This is because it is a vital part of how we reduce carbon dioxide in the atmosphere, which warms the planet. We need to preserve the hundreds of plants, animals, fungi and microscopic organisms that live in the Amazon ecosystem. Also the humans who live there. Not only do the animals get burnt in the fires. But those that survive have their sources of food and natural habitats destroyed, so they may eventually die, even if they survive the fire.*"

"Many native humans in the Amazon lose their homes by fire, but sometimes they also get ill from diseases, like malaria. When the rain forests are destroyed because of the damage to the biodiversity, swamps can emerge where insects that carry diseases can thrive."

Mum continues, "*Unfortunately, we have not only had bad fires in Brazil but also in Australia this year.*"

"In Australia, the bush fires made the sky pink and orange. Fire fighters were overrun by over 1000 degrees C temperature heat. Vast areas of bushland were destroyed including in Queensland. New South Wales was the worst affected state. For 3 years there had been very low rainfall, so the fires spread quickly destroying many unique animal ecosystems. Even though in the arid dry parts of Australia fires do occur each year, the Government said the fires were starting earlier than expected. They were more intense because of the extreme weather that had been occurring in recent years."

"The toxic smoke spread and the famous town of Sydney became consumed in smoke for weeks.

The bush fires in Australia released more carbon than the country's annual carbon dioxide output. The fires tragically mean that not only do people lose their homes and families, but also there is loss of work and profits to live on."

"This shows that Australia seems to also be at the forefront of the global climate change emergency, which we protested about at the Houses of Parliament," says Tom.

Mum reports, *"Another fire which became extreme was the fire in Paradise town, in California, in 2018. This has been the deadliest most destructive fire there in history. There were always fires in the area, but none so extreme. Paradise was known for its beautiful tall trees and humming birds, butterflies and mountains."*

This previous fire was also reported on in the news bulletin. Mum commented, "This fire may have started from electrical sparks 7 miles away from the town. But the extreme weather conditions including the strong high winds, warm temperature and very dry vegetation meant the fire spread extremely rapidly to Paradise town. Climate change resulted in the area having longer summers with drought, no rainfall for many months, high winds and high temperatures. Paradise is now a ghost town with only about 85 residents where formerly 40,000 people lived."

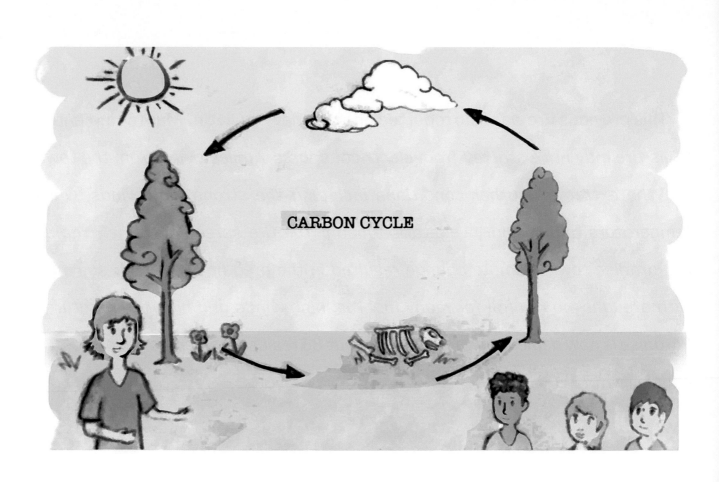

"There is also the problem of toxic fumes from fires you told us about," says Kate

"Yes, well remembered, "remarks Mum. "All the carbon dioxide given off from burning trees in forest fires causes pollution and this is bad for our lungs and can cause breathing problems. It also warms the atmosphere causing it to heat up producing climate change. But the animals and plants that have normally lived together die as their ecosystem is destroyed. This is destroying our biodiversity essential to life on earth.

What did we learn today? (tick the box if you understood and agree)

☐ Very extreme temperatures and dry weather caused by climate change has caused catastrophic fires to sweep across the land and destroy plants and animals, especially in the Amazon and in Australia.

☐ The Amazon and Australian fires caused much damage and raged for many weeks.

☐ Governments need to take action quickly to reduce these fires happening again and this will take co-operation across the world.

☐ The aim of the Children's Extinction Rebellion is to support plans to reduce carbon emissions to reduce extreme climate change.

Read how Kate and Tom learn about the Antarctic warming in book 13.

Children Saving our Planet Series

Books

1. **Tom and Kate Go to Westminster**

2. **Kate and Tom Learn About Fossil Fuels**

3. **Tom and Kate Chose Green Carbon**

4. **Tress and Deforestation**

5. **Our Neighbourhood Houses**

6. **Our Neighbourhood Roads**

7. **Shopping at the Farm Shop**

8. **Travelling to a Holiday by the Sea**

9. **Picnic at the Seaside on Holiday**

These series of simple books explain the landmark importance of Children's participation in the Extinction rebellion protest. Children actively want to encourage and support adults to urgently tackle both the Climate and the Biodiversity emergencies. The booklets enable children at an early age to understand some of the scientific principles that are affecting the destruction of the planet. If global political and economic systems fail to address the climate emergency, the responsibility will rest upon children to save the Planet for themselves.

This series is dedicated to

Theodore, Aria and Ophelia.

Printed in the United States
by Baker & Taylor Publisher Services

Printed in the United States
by Baker & Taylor Publisher Services